CANDY Cocktails

FUN AND FLIRTY DRINKS WITH A *Sugar-Kissed* TWIST

FLANNERY GOOD AND KATHERINE GOOD

Running Press
PHILADELPHIA · LONDON

Published by Running Press,
A Member of the Perseus Books Group

Books published by Running Press are available at special discounts for bulk purchases in the United States by corporations, institutions, and other organizations. For more information, please contact the Special Markets Department at the Perseus Books Group, 2300 Chestnut Street, Suite 200, Philadelphia, PA 19103, or call (800) 810-4145, ext. 5000, or e-mail special.markets@perseusbooks.com.

ISBN 978-0-7624-5112-8
Library of Congress Control Number: 2013945768

E-book ISBN 978-0-7624-5182-1

9 8 7 6 5 4 3 2 1
Digit on the right indicates the number of this printing

Cover and interior design by Melissa Gerber
Edited by Jordana Tusman
Typography: Core Circus, Thirsty Rough Regular, and ITC Avant Garde Gothic STD

Running Press Book Publishers
2300 Chestnut Street
Philadelphia, PA 19103–4371

Visit us on the web!
www.offthemenublog.com

{ TO MOM AND DAD WITH LOTS OF LOVE }

Contents

CANDY COCKTAILS

Introduction

Greetings! We are the splendidly blonde and often outrageous mixology sisters, Flannery and Katherine Good. Welcome to our colorful candy-coated cocktail world!

When we started our cocktail blog, Fashionably Bombed, we were looking for a way to express our creativity. At the time, most cocktail blogs were serious and most cocktail recipes were boring. We thought to ourselves, Wait! Aren't cocktails supposed to be FUN? So we decided to take it upon ourselves to inject the cocktail world with crazy, colorful concoctions embellished with glitter and candy! We started with two of our favorites, mojitos and margaritas, and from there just let our imaginations run wild. Because we are both major sugar junkies who still dream about lollipops and gumdrops at night, it's not surprising that candy soon made its way into our drinks. And once we started making candy cocktails, we couldn't stop!

Our first creation was a boozy peanut butter cup milkshake for Halloween. This particular drink needed a little tweaking, but we couldn't get the candy cocktail idea out of our heads. Like most kids, we were obsessed with candy, and apparently we never outgrew that phase!

This cocktail book is overflowing with girly, sweet drinks all made from, or made to taste like, your favorite candy! In fact, we've filled the book with so many fun and tasty cocktails that we had a hard time staying sober while writing it!

You'll start by learning how to make your own candy-infused liquor. This is not only an important step in the drink-making process, but it's also crazy-fun. From bubblegum-infused rum to make our Bubblegum Mojito to Altoids-infused bourbon to make our Breath Mint Julep, the liquor and candy combination possibilities are endless.

We've included a sweet candy cocktails chapter where we show you how to make drinks out of yummy things like cotton candy, Red Hots–infused vodka, Nerds, Good & Plenty–infused rum, and Swedish Fish!

We also show you how to make chocolate candy cocktails. These all taste like your favorite chocolate candies, including chocolate covered

cherries, Snickers, and Reese's Peanut Butter Cups. We even invented a chocolate margarita, which, if we do say so ourselves, is super tasty! There's a chapter dedicated to sour candy cocktails, which are our FAVORITES! Here we use things like sour gummy bears, Jelly Belly jelly beans, cherry Jolly Rancher–infused vodka, and Lemonhead candies.

And no cocktail book would be complete without a chapter on shots, but these aren't just any shots—they're candy shots! Gumballs, Pop Rocks, and Skittles shots are all included. The frozen candy cocktails chapter is bursting with milkshakes, daiquiris, and margaritas, all of which are cold, tasty, candy-filled treats! You'll also find our holiday candy cocktails chapter to be fun and festive, with drinks like our Honey Bunny, where you rip off the head of a hollow chocolate Easter bunny and fill its body with a yummy honey-based cocktail.

And last, but not least, is our chapter on how to throw a fabulous candy cocktail party. Once you know how to make the cocktails, we'll show you how to make super-cute garnishes, decorations, and more! So whether you're a chocoholic, a lover of licorice, or a diehard fan of Sour Patch Kids, there's a whole world of boozy candy-coated fun waiting for you in this book!

Glassware

The glass that you choose for your cocktail is just as important as the dress that you pour yourself into before going out on a hot date! A Cotton Candy-tini served in a coffee mug is like you getting your hair and makeup done and then putting on a burlap sack! This chapter is here to make sure that your cocktails are always properly dressed.

BRANDY GLASS: that big mamma jamma that fancy guys smoking cigars swirl their brandy in. It's like a fishbowl with a short stem!

CHAMPAGNE FLUTE: a stem glass with a long, narrow bowl. This glass means it's officially time to celebrate!

COCKTAIL OR MARTINI GLASS: the quintessential cocktail glass. It is cone-shaped with a long stem, and it's what almost every froufrou girly drink comes served in.

COLLINS GLASS: a tall, skinny glass that is great for drinks topped with soda water. It's the glass that keeps your mojito fizzy.

JULEP CUP: a cup traditionally made out of sterling silver, allowing a frost to form on the outside, keeping your drink ice cold. Although you won't be breaking these out everyday, it sure is fancy to have the proper cup when it's mint julep season.

HIGHBALL GLASS: a glass tumbler that is shorter and wider than a collins glass.

MASON JAR: a glass jar traditionally used for canning. It also happens to be a chic way to store your DIY liquor infusions.

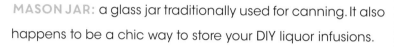

MARGARITA GLASS: a glass with a wide bowl that is perfect for rimming with salt, sugar, or most importantly, crushed candy!

MILKSHAKE GLASS: a tall, classic glass that soda fountains have used for ages. It always looks best with whipped cream on top!

MUG: an old cupboard staple that works well for hot alcoholic drinks.

OLD-FASHIONED OR ROCKS GLASS: a short, wide glass for all those *Mad Men*-esque cocktails.

SHOT GLASS: a small glass that holds about two ounces of liquid. It's the little glass that causes big trouble!

WINE GLASS: stemware that is used to drink and taste wine. It has three main parts: the stem, the bowl, and the foot.

Tools and Equipment

The proper tools are an important part of cocktail making. Without them, even the easiest task will quickly become frustrating. Always keep the following tools and equipment on hand when you're making candy cocktails.

BAR SPOON: a long-handled spoon that is perfect for stirring cocktails. It can also be used to layer drinks.

BLENDER: a necessity for blended and frozen drinks like margaritas and daiquiris.

CITRUS SQUEEZER: a tool used to squeeze the juice from lemons, limes, and oranges.

COCKTAIL SHAKER: the most essential tool for mixing cocktails. We prefer the stainless steel variety with a lid and strainer.

HAWTHORNE STRAINER: if your cocktail shaker doesn't have a built-in strainer, this tool fits nicely on top of the bottom half of any cocktail shaker.

JIGGER: a two-sided tool used to measure your ingredients. In most cases, one side holds one ounce and the other side holds two ounces.

MUDDLER: a tool used to press the flavor, oils, and juices out of ingredients at the bottom of the glass. We use the traditional wooden style. A definite must-have for mojito lovers!

Spirits

One of the things that we love about going to a bar is sitting and staring at all the different liquor bottles against the wall. So many pretty colors and bottle designs! And then, of course, there's what's inside them! Because without the booze, it's not really a cocktail, now is it? Here is a list of some of the essential spirits we use in this book.

BITTERS: concentrated alcohol made from herbs and spices (we prefer Angostura, from Trinidad and Tobago).

BLUE CURAÇAO: a blue liqueur made from the dried peel of the laraha fruit. It has a similar flavor to an orange.

BOURBON: a type of American whiskey made primarily from corn.

BRANDY: a spirit produced by distilling wine; or, it is sometimes made from fermented fruits.

CHAMBORD: a black raspberry liqueur from France.

CHAMPAGNE: a sparkling wine produced from grapes grown in the Champagne region of France.

CRÈME DE CACAO: a chocolate-flavored liqueur sweetened with vanilla.

DRAMBUIE: a sweet, golden-colored liqueur made from malt whiskey, honey, herbs, and spices.

GIN: a grain spirit that derives its flavor from juniper berries.

GODIVA CHOCOLATE LIQUEUR: a chocolate liqueur made with Godiva chocolate. Comes in milk, dark, and white chocolate varieties.

IRISH CREAM: a liqueur made with cream, Irish whiskey, and other ingredients.

JÄGERMEISTER: a German liqueur made from fifty-six herbs, fruits, roots, and spices including citrus peel, licorice, anise, poppy seeds, saffron, ginger, juniper berries, and ginseng.

KAHLUA: a coffee-flavored, rum-based liqueur from Mexico.

RED WINE: a wine made from dark-colored grape varieties.

RUM: a spirit made from fermented sugarcane juice.

SCHNAPPS: a grain spirit mixed with flavors and sugar.

TEQUILA: a Mexican spirit made from the agave plant.

TRIPLE SEC: a colorless orange-flavored liqueur made from dried orange peels.

VODKA: a colorless, distilled spirit made from grains, potatoes, fruit, or sugar.

WHISKEY: a spirit made from fermented grain mash.

Candy Rims and Garnishes

Candy rims and garnishes are to cocktails what icing is to cake! Rimming a glass is really quite easy, and adding a garnish or edible decoration can be a fun way to get creative.

Liquid Rims

CARAMEL, MELTED SQUARES: Unwrap ten caramel squares and cut them into small pieces. Place pieces on a small plate and melt them in the microwave for 30 seconds at a time, stirring in between intervals to ensure they are evenly melted. Once the caramel is melted, dip the rim of the glass directly into the caramel, turning it until the rim is evenly coated. If the recipe calls for a solid rim, then dip the rim immediately into the solid ingredients.

CHOCOLATE, MELTED SQUARES—WHITE, MILK, OR DARK: Using 1 ounce of chocolate per glass, cut chocolate into small bits. Melt the chocolate of choice on a plate in the microwave for 30 seconds at a time, checking and stirring it each time, until fully melted. (But not burnt!) Dip the rim of the glass directly into the chocolate, ensuring that there is an even coating of chocolate around the rim of the glass. Then immediately dip the chocolate rim into the solid rim of your choice, pressing down slightly to ensure that it sticks to the chocolate. Place these rimmed glasses in the refrigerator until you are ready to pour and serve your drinks.

CHOCOLATE OR CARAMEL SYRUP: Pour approximately 2 tablespoons of syrup onto a plate and dip the rim of the glass directly into the syrup. Place rimmed glass in the refrigerator until you are ready to pour and serve your cocktails.

CORN SYRUP: If you want to rim your glass in a heavy ingredient, try rimming it in a light corn syrup first so that the ingredients stick easier.

LIME JUICE: Cut a small lime wedge and slide it around the rim of the glass, twisting the glass so that the entire rim is covered in a thin layer of lime juice. Then dip the wet rim into your desired solid rim (e.g., salt, chili powder, etc.).

Solid Rims

(UNLESS OTHERWISE STATED, USE ⅛ CUP OF EACH INGREDIENT PER GLASS FOR RIMMING.)

Almonds, toasted, chopped

Candy cane, crushed (1 candy cane)

Chili powder mixture (1 tablespoon of course salt plus 1 tablespoon of chili powder)

Chocolate sprinkles

Cinnamon hard candies, crushed

Coconut, sweetened shredded, sometimes toasted

Edible silver glitter stars (½ teaspoon) (Can be found in the cake decorating section of select grocery stores.)

Gold pearlized sugar sprinkles

Heart-shaped sprinkles

Graham cracker crumbs

Green shredded coconut (Make your own by adding 2 to 3 drops of green food coloring to ¼ cup of shredded coconut. Mix well with your hands until the coconut is evenly coated. Use gloves if you don't want green hands!)

Jumbo Rainbow Nonpareils sprinkles, large multicolored

Pink sugar crystals

Peanuts, salted, chopped

Pixy Stix (2 packets)

Pop Rocks (1 packet)

Rock salt

Sour gummy dust (This can be found at the bottom of a package of Sour Patch Kids, or you can make your own by mixing 3 tablespoons of superfine sugar and 1 tablespoon of citric acid. Citric acid can usually be found in the can aisle at most grocery stores.)

Sprinkles, multicolored

Yellow Jimmies

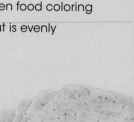

Apple slices, fresh

Black licorice straws

Black licorice wheels

Blow Pops

Candy canes

Chocolate-covered malt balls

Chocolate wafer cookies

Ground nutmeg

Gummy cherries

Gummy raspberries and blackberries

Gummy worms

Heath Toffee Bar, chopped

Hollow chocolate bunnies

Jelly beans

Large gumballs

Maraschino cherries

Marshmallow circus peanuts

Marshmallows, toasted

Mexican lollipops

Mint leaves, fresh

Nerds

Orange slices, candy

Orange slices, fresh

Peppermint Patties

Red wax lips

Reese's Peanut Butter Cups Minis

Root beer barrels

Snickers, bite-sized

Sour Patch Kids

Sunkist fruit gummies

Swedish Fish

Tootsie Roll Pops

Twizzlers Rainbow Twists

Whipped cream

Simple Syrup

A few of the recipes in this book call for simple syrup. Here's an easy recipe so you can make your own.

1 CUP WATER
1 CUP GRANULATED SUGAR

In a medium saucepan, bring the water and sugar to a boil. Stir until the sugar completely dissolves. Let cool. Once the syrup reaches room temperature, add to cocktails. You can store remainder in the refrigerator for up to one month.

Candy Liquor Infusions

Put on your lab coat and safety goggles and grab as much booze and candy as you can, because this, ladies and gents, is the first step in your candy cocktail adventure! Many of the cocktails in this book include candy liquor infusions. It may seem intimidating at first, but once you start you'll see how easy it is to whip up these DIY concoctions. Before you know it you'll be showing off your skills by inventing your own unique combos. And when you do, be sure to let us know if you come up with any good ones!

STEP #1: Add 10 pieces (or ¼ cup) of candy to a mason jar.

STEP #2: Add ½ cup liquor (rum, vodka, gin, tequila, etc.).

STEP #3: Close the lid and shake.

Your infusion should be ready in as little as twenty-four hours or as long as one week, depending on the consistency of the candy. Candy corn, for example, will be ready within twenty-four hours, whereas bubblegum infusions take about one week to get the full flavor. Experiment with different candies and liquors, and taste test your infusions to determine when they're ready to use.

Infusions used in this book

VODKA INFUSIONS

Caramel vodka (page 106)

Altoids vodka (pages 48 and 56)

Lemonhead vodka (page 102)

Bubblegum vodka (pages 108 and 114)

Red Hots vodka (page 26)

Marshmallow vodka (page 62)

Strawberry Starburst vodka (page 100)

Apple Jolly Rancher vodka (pages 68 and 120)

Cherry Jolly Rancher vodka (pages 52 and 114)

Nips vodka (page 112)

Skittles vodka (page 110)

Candy corn vodka (page 126)

Conversation heart vodka (only include the pink, orange, and yellow hearts, otherwise the color will be brown—not a good look!) (page 118)

BRANDY INFUSIONS

Grape Jolly Rancher brandy (page 76)

TEQUILA INFUSIONS

Red Hots tequila (page 96)

Cherry Jolly Rancher tequila (page 70)

Banana Runts tequila (page 38)

Watermelon Jolly Rancher tequila (page 92)

WHISKEY INFUSIONS

Altoids bourbon (page 86)

Choward's Violet Mints whiskey (page 36)

RUM INFUSIONS

Good & Plenty rum (page 28)

Lemonhead rum (page 72)

Bubblegum rum (page 24)

GIN INFUSIONS

Blue raspberry Jolly Rancher gin (page 78)

Choward's Guava gin (page 80)

CANDY COCKTAILS

Sweet Candy Cocktails

I t wouldn't be a candy cocktail book without featuring cocktails made out of sweet candy, now would it? Whether you're a fan of bubble gum or licorice, cotton candy or circus peanuts, this is the perfect chapter to get your sweet-tooth fix!

23

Bubblegum Mojito

Every summer we get on a crazy mojito kick and start mixing in everything we can get our hot little hands on. One year, after running out of fresh seasonal fruit options (like strawberries, peaches, and cherries), we hit up our candy drawer (more like a closet, really!) and this tasty little number was born.

1 ounce fresh lime juice

1 ounce simple syrup (page 20)

10 sprigs fresh mint, plus 1 sprig for garnish

2 ounces bubblegum rum infusion (page 20)

Dash of grenadine

Soda water, to top

2 large bubblegum balls, for garnish

Muddle the lime juice, simple syrup, and 10 mint sprigs in a highball glass. Add the rum infusion and grenadine and stir. Add crushed ice and top with soda water. Garnish with a skewer of the bubblegum balls and the mint sprig.

Candy Apple Cocktail

Every year when the fair comes to town we get all jacked up on soft tacos and corn dogs and start fantasizing about inventing things like deep-fried Rum and Coke balls. (Just kidding! Sort of. . . .) So last year while looking for a way to use our Red Hots vodka, we tried mixing in some hard apple cider and, well, the fair may have left town, but we're still enjoying the ride!

Corn syrup, for rim

Cinnamon hard candies, for rim

½ ounce Red Hots vodka infusion (page 20)

Hard apple cider, to top (we like Woodchuck)

Red apple slice, for garnish

Dab corn syrup onto the rim of a champagne flute and then dip the rim in crushed cinnamon hard candies. Pour the vodka infusion into the flute. Top with chilled hard apple cider. Gently stir. Garnish with the thin red apple slice.

Black Licorice Mojito

Mojitos make everything better. Just sayin'. Even if you don't think you're a black licorice fan, you might just find yourself asking for another round of these babies. There is something quite amazing about the combination of mint, lime, and Good & Plenty rum.

1 ounce fresh lime juice

1 ounce simple syrup (page 20)

10 sprigs fresh mint, plus 1 sprig for garnish

2 ounces Good & Plenty rum infusion (page 20)

Soda water, to top

Black licorice straw, for garnish

Muddle the lime juice, simple syrup, and 10 sprigs of mint in a highball glass. Add the rum infusion and stir. Add crushed ice and top with the soda water. Garnish with the licorice straw—with both ends cut off—and the mint sprig.

Cotton Candy-tini

While we are huge fans of our local county fair, we are even bigger fans of the cotton candy they serve. Thanks to this little invention we like to call the Cotton Candy-tini, now you, too, can relive the magic of the fair all year long.

1 cup pink cotton candy, loosely packed

2 ounces vodka

2 ounces butterscotch schnapps

1 ounce fresh lemon juice

Put the cotton candy into a martini glass. In a shaker with ice, add vodka, butterscotch schnapps, and lemon juice. Shake and strain into the martini glass.

Candy Fishbowl

This has to be hands down the cutest candy cocktail we've made to date. It's so cute, in fact, that you might not want to drink it for fear of ruining the lovely little masterpiece. But trust us, once you take a sip, you won't be able to stop drinking until it's all gone.

3 ounces coconut rum (we like Malibu)

½ ounce Blue Curaçao

1 cup pineapple juice

¼ cup Nerds

2 to 3 Swedish Fish

Add rum, curaçao, and pineapple juice to a shaker with ice. Shake well and pour into a brandy glass. Add enough Nerds to fill a quarter inch of the bottom of the glass. Add the Swedish Fish to the bottom of the glass and garnish with one Swedish Fish.

Chocolate Orange Lollipop

Back in the day, when we used to go trick-or-treating, Tootsie Roll Pops were high on the Halloween candy exchange list. Our favorite flavor was orange, so we decided to create a cocktail that tastes just like an orange Tootsie Roll Pop!

2 ounces fresh orange juice

1 ounce crème de cacao

1 ounce vanilla vodka

½ ounce orange liqueur

½ ounce fresh lemon juice

1 orange Tootsie Roll Pop, for garnish

Add all the ingredients, except for the garnish, in a shaker with ice. Shake vigorously and pour in a cocktail glass. Garnish with the orange Tootsie Roll Pop.

Violet Old-Fashioned

After an intense all-night *Mad Men* rerun session, we were inspired to make this candy version of the traditional Old-Fashioned! And we couldn't think of a candy that was more old-fashioned than Choward's Violet Mints. Warning: This floral number might just be the most manly candy cocktail we've ever invented, so man up!

1 to 2 dashes bitters (we like Angostura)

1 maraschino cherry, plus 1 for garnish

1 candy orange slice, plus 1 for garnish

2 ounces Choward's Violet Mints whiskey infusion (page 20)

Soda water, to top

Muddle the bitters, 1 maraschino cherry, and 1 orange slice in the bottom of an old-fashioned glass. Add the whiskey infusion and ice, then top with the soda water. Garnish with the remaining maraschino cherry and orange slice.

Circus Peanut Margarita

Step right up! This is your chance to drink—yes, drink—an orange peanut-shaped marshmallow. We've been fascinated with these candies since we were really young, probably because our mom wouldn't ever let us get them (turns out she didn't like them!), but also because in the candy world banana-flavored things are usually yellow, not orange!

Corn syrup, for rim

Multicolored sprinkles, for rim

3 ounces Banana Runts tequila infusion (page 20)

2 ounces fresh lime juice

Dash of grenadine

A few circus peanuts, for garnish

Rim a margarita glass with corn syrup and dip the rim in multicolored sprinkles, then set aside. Shake the rest of the ingredients with ice in a cocktail shaker. Strain over ice into the rocks glass and garnish with the circus peanuts on a skewer.

Pimm's Candy Cup

This traditional English cocktail just got a candy cocktail makeover. We've taken out the traditional fresh fruit and cucumber slices and replaced them with some yummy fruit gummies. Cheers, mate!

¼ cup Sunkist Fruit Gummies, reserving 3 to 4 for garnish

2 ounces Pimm's

1 ounce fresh lemon juice

1 cup lemon-lime soda

Add ¼ cup of fruit gummies to the bottom of a highball glass. Add the Pimm's, lemon juice, and lemon-lime soda. Top with ice cubes and garnish with 3 to 4 fruit gummies on a stick.

Berry Goodie Gumdrop

While perusing the candy aisle of our local grocery store, we discovered the cutest little gummy raspberries and blackberries. They inspired us to make this berry delicious version of the gumdrop martini. Yum!

2 ounces Chambord

2 ounces vodka

2 ounces fresh lemon juice

A few gummy raspberries and blackberries, for garnish

Add all the ingredients to a cocktail shaker and shake well. Pour into a martini glass and garnish with gummy raspberries and blackberries.

CANDY COCKTAILS

Chocolate Candy Cocktails

Who doesn't love the candy bar aisle in the grocery store? Chocolate, caramel, peanuts, toffee—what more could a girl ask for? There's only one thing that could make it even better . . . booze! Well, lucky you, this chapter is dedicated to boozy versions of your favorite classic chocolate candy bars!

Salted Chocolate Margarita

Move over margarita, there's a new sheriff in town—the Salted Chocolate Margarita. This is a great margarita for chocolate lovers. The salted rim perfectly complements the sweet rich chocolaty flavor of the margarita.

Chocolate syrup, for rim (page 17)

Rock salt, for rim

1½ ounces heavy whipping cream

1½ ounces crème de cacao

1 ounce tequila

1 ounce chocolate syrup

¼ ounce triple sec

Rim a margarita glass with chocolate syrup and rock salt, and set it aside. Pour all the ingredients into a blender over roughly 1½ cups ice and blend well, for about 1 to 2 minutes, or until slushy. Pour into the margarita glass.

Peppermint Patt-ini

If you think eating those round discs of dark-chocolate covered minty goodness is refreshing, wait until you drink this. *Brrrrr!* This is literally the liquid version of that classic silver-wrapped treat.

Dark chocolate, melted, for rim (page 16)

Edible silver glitter stars, for rim

3 ounces heavy whipping cream

2 ounces Altoids vodka infusion (page 20)

1 sprig fresh mint, for garnish

1 Peppermint Pattie, for garnish

Rim a martini glass with melted dark chocolate and edible silver glitter stars, and set aside. Shake the rest of the ingredients with ice in a cocktail shaker. Strain into the martini glass. Garnish with the mint sprig and the Peppermint Pattie.

Peanut Butter Cup

A few years ago we got crazy and decided that we should make a drink out of our favorite Halloween candy. So we jammed a bunch of Reese's Peanut Butter Cups into a blender and added a bunch of booze. Fortunately for you, we reworked the recipe and realized that sometimes you just need the drink to taste like candy, rather than putting the *actual* candy in the drink.

Milk chocolate, melted, for rim (page 16)

Crushed chocolate wafer cookies, for rim

¼ cup salted crunchy peanut butter

¼ cup whole milk

½ ounce vodka

1 ounce crème de cacao

4 to 6 Reese's Peanut Butter Cups Minis, for garnish

Rim a martini glass with melted milk chocolate and then with crushed chocolate wafer cookies, and set aside. Combine the peanut butter, milk, vodka, and crème de cacao in a blender until smooth. Shake mixture with ice in a cocktail shaker and strain into the martini glass. Garnish with the stack of mini peanut butter cups.

Chocolate-Covered Cherry

Are we the only ones who got in trouble for biting into every piece of candy in the box until we found the chocolate-covered cherry? Well, we're all grown up now, thank you very much, and we don't have to sneak around anymore. Now we drink our candy like adults!

Milk chocolate, melted, for rim (page 16)

Crushed cherry Jolly Ranchers, for rim

1 ounce crème de cacao

1 ounce cherry Jolly Rancher vodka infusion (page 20)

1 ounce heavy whipping cream

1 maraschino cherry, for garnish

Rim a martini glass with melted milk chocolate and crushed cherry Jolly Ranchers and set it aside. Combine the crème de cacao, vodka infusion, and cream over ice in a cocktail shaker. Shake and then strain into the martini glass. Garnish with the maraschino cherry.

Liquid Candy Bar

It's the quintessential candy bar full of chocolate, caramel, and peanutty goodness in the form of a drink. We can't claim that it's any lower in calories, but it has a certain feel-good effect that the real thing definitely doesn't.

Caramel squares, melted and then cooled, for rim (page 16)

Salted peanuts, finely chopped, for rim

1 ounce heavy whipping cream

1 ounce vanilla vodka

1 ounce crème de cacao

4 to 6 Snickers Minis, for garnish

Rim a martini glass with melted caramel and finely chopped salted peanuts and set it aside. Shake the whipping cream, vodka, and crème de cacao with ice in a cocktail shaker. Strain into the martini glass. Garnish with the Snickers Minis on a skewer.

Minty Fresh Hot Chocolate

Can you think of a better flavor combination than mint and chocolate? We can't! Which is why we invented the perfect candy cocktail for a cold winter's day. And after you're done with your drink, your breath will be minty fresh.

1 cup whole milk

4 ounces milk chocolate, cut into tiny pieces

2 ounces Altoids vodka infusion (page 20)

Whipped cream, for garnish

1 sprig fresh mint, for garnish

In a small saucepan, warm the milk and chocolate over medium heat, stirring constantly. Continue stirring until the chocolate is fully dissolved, about 2 minutes, then remove it from the heat and stir in the vodka infusion. Pour the mixture in a mug and garnish with whipped cream and the mint sprig.

Coconut Joy Martini

Sometimes you feel like a nut, sometimes you don't . . . but you always feel like a cocktail! Let's face it: There are some things that are just made to go together. Three of those things—chocolate, coconut, and almonds—can be found in this super tasty cocktail.

Milk chocolate, melted, for rim (page 16)

Toasted almonds, finely chopped, for rim

2 ounces coconut cream

2 ounces crème de cacao

1 ounce vodka

Toasted coconut, for garnish

Rim a martini glass with melted milk chocolate and then with finely chopped toasted almonds, and set it aside. Shake coconut cream, crème de cacao, and vodka with ice in a cocktail shaker. Strain into the martini glass. Garnish with a sprinkling of the toasted coconut on top.

Dirt-y Martini

Our version of this cocktail definitely beats an ordinary dirty martini. After one sip of this chocolaty dirty version, you'll never look at dirt and worms the same way again.

Chocolate syrup, for rim (page 17)

Crushed chocolate wafers, for rim

1 ounce Godiva Chocolate Liqueur

½ ounce Kahlua

1 ounce Baileys Irish Cream

1½ ounces heavy whipping cream

Pinch of salt

3 to 4 gummy worms, for garnish

Rim a martini glass in chocolate syrup and then crushed chocolate wafers, and set it aside. Pour the remaining ingredients, including the salt, into a cocktail shaker with ice and shake vigorously. Pour the mixture into the martini glass and garnish with gummy worms.

S'more-tini

We must admit, we're not big on "roughing it" in the great outdoors, but our love of s'mores almost makes us wish we were. That's why we invented the s'mores-tini. It's like "glamping"—glamorous camping—for cocktailistas!

Milk chocolate, melted, for rim (page 16)

Graham cracker crumbs, for rim

2 ounces heavy whipping cream

2 ounces marshmallow vodka infusion (page 20)

1 ounce crème de cacao

½ ounce chocolate syrup

Pinch of salt

1 toasted marshmallow, for garnish

Rim a martini glass in melted milk chocolate and graham cracker crumbs, and set it aside. In a shaker with ice, pour the cream, vodka infusion, crème de cacao, chocolate syrup, and salt. Shake vigorously and pour the mixture into the martini glass. Garnish with the toasted marshmallow.

CANDY COCKTAILS

Sour Candy Cocktails

This is by far our favorite chapter! As kids when we went to the candy store, we would immediately head to the sour section, grabbing all our favorites like Sour Patch Kids, Lemonheads, and sour jelly beans. So pucker up, buttercup, because this chapter is super sour!

Whiskey Sour Gummy Bear

If we could only eat one candy for the rest of our lives, it would probably be sour gummy anything! Although the classic Whiskey Sour is a pretty delicious drink that doesn't really need much tweaking, a sprinkling of sour gummy dust (a.k.a. the citric acid at the bottom of the bag) on the rim gives it a little extra punch in the face!

Lime juice, for rim

Sour gummy dust, for rim (page 18)

1½ ounces fresh lemon juice

1½ ounces whiskey

¾ ounce simple syrup (page 20)

4 to 6 Sour Patch Kids, for garnish

Rim a rocks glass with lime juice and sour gummy dust (you can use the sour dust from Sour Patch Kids), and set it aside. Shake the rest of the ingredients with ice in a cocktail shaker. Strain the mixture into the rocks glass. Garnish with a skewer of the Sour Patch Kids.

Caramel Apple Fizz

This drink is based on one of our favorite sweet county fair treats: the caramel apple. But watch out, because the caramel rim is so tasty, you might accidently bite the glass.

4 caramel squares, melted, for rim (page 16)

1½ ounces apple Jolly Rancher vodka infusion (page 20)

½ ounce fresh lemon juice

Soda water, to top

Rim a highball glass with melted caramel and set it aside. Add the vodka infusion, lemon juice, and some ice to the glass, then top with soda water, and stir briefly.

Sour Cherry Margarita

Cherry Jolly Ranchers have to be one of the best candies for making alcohol infusions. After inventing cherry Jolly Rancher tequila, we decided the best use of this new infusion would be a sour cherry margarita—and boy were we right on the money!

Lime juice, for rim

Pink sugar crystals, for rim

1 ounce cherry Jolly Rancher tequila infusion (page 20)

1 ounce fresh lime juice

½ ounce triple sec

2 to 3 gummy cherries, for garnish

Rim a margarita glass with lime juice and then dip in pink sugar crystals. Pour tequila infusion, fresh lime juice, and triple sec into a shaker of ice and shake well. Pour into the margarita glass and garnish with the gummy cherries.

Sour Lemon Drop Mojito

While writing this book, we started to wonder, What couldn't you put in a mojito?? This is a super refreshing twist on the original Cuban classic using—yep, you guessed it—Lemonhead infused rum.

10 sprigs fresh mint, plus 1 sprig for garnish

2 ounces Lemonhead infused rum (page 20)

1 ounce fresh lime juice

Soda water, to top

Muddle the 10 sprigs of mint, rum infusion, and lime juice in a mixing glass. Pour over crushed ice in a highball glass. Top with soda water and garnish with the mint sprig.

Jelly Bell-ini

As little girls our favorite aunt took us on a tour of the Jelly Belly factory. We were already huge fans of Jelly Belly jelly beans, but this trip made us fans for life. Now that we're adults we've found the perfect way to combine one of our favorite childhood candies with a classic adult beverage—the Bellini! And it tastes just like a peach-flavored Jelly Belly!

1 ounce peach schnapps

1 ounce fresh lemon juice

Champagne, to top

5 to 6 peach Jelly Belly jelly beans, for garnish

Pour the peach schnapps and lemon juice into a champagne flute. Top with the champagne. Garnish with the peach Jelly Belly jelly beans stacked on a skewer.

Sour Grape Sidecar

If you're as big a sour fanatic as we are, then this is definitely the drink for you. We've turned this otherwise boring WWI cocktail into a sour grape extravaganza. And best of all, we've even rimmed it with a grape flavored Pixy Stix.

1 fresh lemon wedge, for rim

2 grape Pixy Stix, for rim

2 ounces grape Jolly Rancher brandy infusion (page 20)

1 ounce fresh lemon juice

½ ounce orange liqueur

1 candy orange slice, for garnish

Rim a martini glass with the lemon wedge and then dip it in the grape Pixy Stix powder and set aside. Add the brandy infusion, fresh lemon juice, and liqueur into a cocktail shaker with ice and shake vigorously. Strain into the martini glass and garnish with the candy orange slice.

Blue Diamond Fizz

Based on the Diamond Fizz, a champagne and gin based cocktail, this is the perfect drink for the girl who loves jewels. Since we have always loved Ring Pops, we figured that they would make the perfect edible garnishes. Serve these at your friend's bachelorette party!

2 ounces blue raspberry Jolly Rancher gin infusion (page 20)

½ ounce fresh lemon juice

Champagne, to top

1 blue Ring Pop, for garnish

Add the gin infusion and lemon juice to a cocktail shaker with ice. Shake well and strain into a champagne flute. Top with the champagne and garnish with the blue Ring Pop.

Guava Gin Rickey

Apparently one day back in the 1890s the Gin Rickey was invented. Yada yada yada, a hundred-plus years go by, and then we come along and make it even better! While out on a recent candy hunting expedition we discovered Choward's Guava candy mints. These are called candy mints, even though they aren't mint flavor. We brought them home and started experimenting. Turns out, they're fantastic with gin.

Lime juice, for rim

Pink sugar crystals, for rim

1 ounce Choward's Guava gin infusion (page 20)

1 ounce fresh lime juice

Soda water, to top

Rim a collins glass with lime juice and then pink sugar. Fill the glass with ice. Add the gin infusion and lime juice, and stir. Top with soda water.

CANDY COCKTAILS

Frozen Candy Cocktails

Whether you're throwing a summer cocktail party or just lounging around the pool, this is the perfect chapter for those hot summer months when all you want to do is cool off! Put on your bikini and get ready to chill—literally!

Adult Root Beer Float

Nothing says summer like a nice cold frothy root beer float. Is there anything better than root beer and ice cream? Two things, actually: the addition of vodka and candy! Now kick off your flip-flops and reeeeeeeelax!

2 ounces vanilla vodka

2 scoops vanilla ice cream

Root beer, to top

Whipped cream, for garnish

5 to 7 root beer barrel candies, crushed, for garnish

Pour the vanilla vodka into a chilled glass mug. Add the ice cream, top with root beer, and stir gently. Garnish with whipped cream and crushed root beer barrels.

Breath Mint Julep

Don't let the name turn you off. This is a very tasty drink that will leave you with fresh breath long after the drink is gone. And although we've never actually been to the Kentucky Derby, we're pretty sure we'd be great at it. After all, we wear big hats all year round and we can do fabulous southern accents. Hey y'all!

3 scoops vanilla ice cream

2 ounces Altoids bourbon infusion (page 20)

¼ cup Junior Mints

1 sprig fresh mint, for garnish

Combine all the ingredients in a blender and blend for 2 minutes, or until smooth. Pour into a silver julep cup. Garnish with the mint sprig.

50/50 Pixy

Ah, remember back to 1952? Yeah, we don't either. But that doesn't mean we can't celebrate one of the best things that happened that year—the invention of Pixy Stix! We decided to combine one of our favorite candy inventions with one of our favorite ice cream inventions: Pixy Stix with the half orange, half vanilla 50/50 bar.

White chocolate, melted, for rim (page 16)

Orange sprinkles, for rim

3 scoops vanilla ice cream

2 ounces vanilla vodka

3 tablespoons frozen orange juice concentrate

Whipped cream, for garnish

1 orange Pixy Stix, for garnish

Rim a milkshake glass with white chocolate and then with orange sprinkles, and set it aside. Combine the ice cream, vodka, and orange juice concentrate in a blender. Blend for 2 minutes, or until smooth. Pour into the glass and top with whipped cream and 1 orange Pixy Stix.

Toffee Bar Beer Float

We know what you're thinking: Beer + candy = gross! But wait, give it a chance. We've managed to convert even the staunchest beer haters with this amazing toffee bar beer float.

3 scoops chocolate ice cream

½ a 22-ounce bottle of chocolate stout

Chocolate syrup, for garnish (page 17)

1 Heath Toffee Bar, chopped, for garnish

Add three scoops of chocolate ice cream to a chilled glass mug. Slowly pour in the chocolate stout. Garnish with the chocolate syrup and chopped Heath Toffee Bar.

Mexican Watermelon Lollipop Margarita

This cocktail was inspired by a recent family trip we took to visit our grandfather's ancestral homeland of Zacatecas. We were especially intrigued by these super spicy chili powder-dipped watermelon lollipops, and soon discovered a way to make a cocktail version of this Mexican treat.

Lime juice, for rim
Chili powder mixture, for rim (page 17)
¼ cup watermelon Jolly Rancher tequila infusion (page 20)
¼ cup fresh lime juice
1 tablespoon granulated sugar (or more, to taste)
⅛ cup triple sec
10 ice cubes
1 Mexican watermelon lollipop, for garnish (found in the Latin American section of the grocery store)

Rim a margarita glass with lime juice, then dip in chili powder mixture and set it aside. Add all the ingredients except the lollipop into a blender and blend for 2 to 3 minutes, or until smooth. Pour into the margarita glass and garnish with the lollipop.

Boozy Malt Ball Shake

Does anyone actually like malt balls? Thanks to this boozy version of the 1950s classic, the malt ball shake, we've become malt ball fans! So put on your poodle skirt and cardigan and do the twist while you down this delicious old-school treat!

½ cup whole milk

¼ cup chocolate-covered malt balls, coarsely chopped, plus a few extras for garnish

¼ cup malted milk powder

2 ounces vanilla vodka

4 scoops vanilla or chocolate ice cream

Add all the ingredients to a blender and blend for 2 minutes, or until smooth. Pour into a milkshake glass and garnish with the extra chopped chocolate malt balls.

Red Hot Kiss Margarita

Come here! This drink wants to give you a big, hot, cinnamony smooch! This drink is sweet, sour, and spicy all rolled into one. And the best part? The sassy red wax lips for garnish. No need for lip injections! Kisses!

Lime juice, for rim

Crushed cinnamon hard candies, for rim

2 ounces Red Hots tequila infusion (page 20)

2 ounces fresh lime juice

1 ounce triple sec

1 red wax lips, for garnish

Rim a margarita glass with lime juice, then dip it in crushed cinnamon hard candies and set it aside. Combine the tequila infusion, lime juice, triple sec, and 2 to 3 cups of ice in a blender. Blend for 2 to 3 minutes, until smooth. Pour into a milkshake glass and garnish with the wax lips.

CANDY COCKTAILS

Candy Shots

There's no better way to get the par-tay started than with shots! Unfortunately, more often than not, drinking them is pure torture. Fortunately for you, the shots in this chapter are so good you might just want to forgo the traditional frat house method and, instead, sip them like a lady.

Neapolitan Coconut Sundae Shot

Remember those little chewy triple layered pink, white, and brown Neapolitan candies? Well, we've made a shot that tastes—dare we say it—better than the real thing!

Melted white chocolate, for rim (page 16)

Shredded coconut, toasted, for rim

½ coconut milk

½ ounce coconut rum

1 ounce strawberry Starburst vodka infusion (page 20)

1 ounce Godiva Chocolate Liqueur

Rim a shot glass in melted white chocolate, then dip it in the shredded coconut and set it aside. In a small bowl, mix together the coconut milk and coconut rum and set the mixture aside. Pour the vodka infusion into the shot glass. Then, using the back of a spoon, gently pour the liqueur in a layer on top, being careful not to mix it with the vodka layer. Finally, using the back of a spoon, slowly pour the rum mixture in a layer on top.

Sour Lemon Drop Shot

What we've got here is the simplest and tastiest shot you've probably ever had: super lemony and sweet at the same time. Be careful, though, it's easy to have one too many of these!

1 fresh lemon wedge, for rim

Yellow Jimmies, for rim

1 ounce fresh lemon juice

1 ounce Lemonhead vodka infusion (page 20)

Rim a shot glass with the lemon wedge, then dip it in yellow polka-dot sprinkles and set it aside. Shake the lemon juice and vodka infusion in a cocktail shaker with ice and strain into the shot glass.

Pop Shot

Pop Rocks have to be the most iconic '80s candy of all time. We knew we had to include at least one Pop Rocks drink in this book because they're just so much fun! This shot tastes so good it hurts.

Lime juice, for rim

1 tablespoon Pop Rocks, for rim, plus a few more for garnish

½ ounce vodka

½ ounce raspberry liqueur

½ ounce fresh lime juice

¼ ounce simple syrup (page 20)

Rim a shot glass with lime juice and Pop Rocks and set it aside. Shake the vodka, raspberry liqueur, lime juice, and simple syrup vigorously with ice in a cocktail shaker and strain into the shot glass. Drop the few remaining Pop Rocks into the shot glass as a garnish and listen to your shot pop!

Money Shot

Made with caramel and peanuts, this is the perfect drink to celebrate payday. Caramel infused vodka, cream with a salted peanut rim—it's money in the bank!

Caramel squares, melted, for rim (page 16)

Salted peanuts, crushed, for rim

1 ounce caramel vodka infusion (page 20)

1 ounce heavy whipping cream

Rim a shot glass with melted caramel and crushed peanuts and set it aside. Shake the caramel vodka and cream with ice in a cocktail shaker. Strain the mixture into the shot glass.

Pink Bubblegum Shot

We are straight-up obsessed with bubblegum. We smack it, wear it (see our bubblegum necklaces on page 142), and decorate with it. So when we made our first batch of DIY bubblegum infused vodka, it sparked a frenzy of bubblegum cocktail making madness! This is a cool and creamy shot with a festive white chocolate and colorful sprinkle rim.

White chocolate, melted, for rim (page 16)

Jumbo rainbow nonpareils sprinkles, for rim (page 18)

1 ounce heavy whipping cream

1 ounce bubblegum vodka infusion (page 20)

Rim a shot glass with melted white chocolate and then dip it in the sprinkles. Shake the cream and vodka infusion with ice in a cocktail shaker and strain the mixture into the shot glass.

Candy Rainbow Shots

Who doesn't love rainbows? This set of colorful rainbow shots looks as good as it tastes!

Makes 5 shots

5 Twizzlers Rainbow Twists, for garnish

RED SHOT

1½ ounces red Skittles vodka infusion (page 20)

1 ounce fresh lemon juice

ORANGE SHOT

1½ ounces orange Skittles vodka infusion (page 20)

1 ounce fresh lemon juice

YELLOW SHOT

1½ ounces yellow Skittles vodka infusion (page 20)

1 ounce fresh lemon juice

GREEN SHOT

1½ ounces green Skittles vodka infusion (page 20)

1 ounce fresh lemon juice

PURPLE SHOT

1½ ounces purple Skittles vodka infusion (page 20)

1 ounce fresh lemon juice

Pour the vodka infusion and lemon juice into a cocktail shaker with ice and shake well. Strain and pour into a shot glass. Repeat for each of the other four shots. Garnish each shot with the appropriate colored Twizzlers Rainbow Twist straw.

White Chocolate Russian Shot

This is the perfect shot for coffee lovers. It tastes just like the classic white Russian we all know and love, only with hints of white chocolate and butterscotch! *Nostrovia!*

White chocolate, melted, for rim (page 16)

Chocolate sprinkles, for rim

1 ounce white chocolate liqueur

1 ounce Nips vodka infusion (page 20)

Rim a shot glass with melted white chocolate and then dip it in the chocolate sprinkles. Shake the liqueur and vodka vigorously with ice in a cocktail shaker and strain the mixture into the shot glass.

Cherry Bubblegum Lollipop Shot

This shot tastes surprisingly like the real thing. It's just like that moment while eating a Blow Pop when you finally break through to the layer of bubblegum, and it mixes perfectly with the sour cherry candy!

½ ounce cherry Jolly Rancher vodka infusion (page 20)

½ ounce bubblegum vodka infusion (page 20)

½ ounce fresh lemon juice

1 Blow Pop, for garnish

Add all the ingredients except the Blow Pop to a cocktail shaker and shake vigorously. Strain into a shot glass and garnish with the Blow Pop.

CANDY COCKTAILS

Holiday Candy Cocktails

Getting dressed up and hosting parties? It's why we get up in the morning! There is nothing that we love more than creating holiday cocktails. We've put our favorite holiday candy cocktails together in this chapter so you can get festive and show off your cocktail-making skills at the same time.

Conversation Heart-tini

Remember Valentine's Day in elementary school? When you had to give everyone a valentine card—even yucky boys! But the best part? Conversation hearts! Valentine's Day just isn't complete without a handful or two of these classic treats.

Lime juice, for rim

Heart-shaped sprinkles, for rim

2 ounces conversation heart vodka infusion (page 20)

1 ounce fresh orange juice

1 ounce fresh lemon juice

Rim a martini glass with lime juice and then heart-shaped sprinkles and set it aside. Shake all the ingredients with ice in a cocktail shaker and strain the mixture into the martini glass.

Pot of Goldschläger

This is the ultimate St. Patrick's Day shot. The apple Jolly Rancher vodka gives this shot a nice green hue and the cinnamon Goldschläger makes it taste like an apple pie!

Lime juice, for rim

Gold pearlized sugar sprinkles, for rim

1 ounce apple Jolly Rancher vodka infusion (page 20)

1 ounce Goldschläger

1 ounce fresh lemon juice

Rim a shot glass with lime juice and gold pearlized sugar and set it aside. Shake all the ingredients with ice in a cocktail shaker and then strain the mixture into the shot glass.

Honey Bunny

Let's face it, the holidays are stressful. That's why we invented this tasty and therapeutic cocktail. When your family starts getting to you, just grab a chocolate bunny, rip its head off, and fill it up with this tasty treat. You'll be feeling better in no time!

1 hollow chocolate bunny (to be used as a cocktail glass)

2 ounces heavy whipping cream

2 ounces Godiva Chocolate Liqueur

2 ounces vanilla vodka

2 ounces Drambuie

Break the head off the bunny. Pour the rest of the ingredients into a cocktail shaker full of ice and shake it. Strain the mixture into the body of the hollow chocolate bunny.

Chocolate Easter Eggnog

Inspired by the Cadbury Creme Egg, we took an easy eggnog recipe and added a chocolate twist. But the best part about it has to be the green "grass" rim. This year the Easter Bunny left you a basket of liquid treats!

White chocolate, melted, for rim (page 16)

Green shredded coconut, for rim

4 ounces heavy whipping cream

1 large egg

1 ounce bourbon

1 ounce crème de cacao

1 tablespoon granulated sugar

¼ teaspoon vanilla extract

A pinch of powdered nutmeg, for garnish

4 to 6 jelly beans, for garnish

Rim a martini glass with melted white chocolate and green coconut and set it aside. Combine the cream, egg, bourbon, crème de cacao, sugar, and vanilla in a blender for 1 to 2 minutes, or until smooth. Refrigerate this mixture for at least 1 hour. Pour into the glass and garnish with nutmeg and the jelly beans on a skewer.

Note: The alcohol in the cocktail kills most of the egg's harmful bacteria, but you might want to consider using pasteurized eggs if you're worried.

Candy Corn Martini

If they sold this sweet Halloween treat year-round we would each weigh three hundred pounds! It's so good that we had to make an infusion with it. We played around with several recipes, but we liked this one best because it's got a nice sweet and sour balance.

Lime juice, for rim

Yellow, orange, and white Jimmies, for rim

1 ounce candy corn vodka infusion (page 20)

1 ounce fresh lemon juice

½ ounce Drambuie

Rim a martini glass with lime juice and the polka-dot sprinkles and set it aside. Shake the rest of the ingredients with ice in a cocktail shaker and then strain the mixture into the glass.

Black Licorice Widow

We love Halloween. In fact, last year we dressed up as life-sized cocktail glasses. (What else?) This year we wanted to make a drink that's super festive and a little different than our other cocktails. So for all you black licorice fans out there, this one's for you. And if you're not a fan, well, we have lots of other cocktails for you!

2 ounces black vodka

1 ounce Jägermeister

1 ounce blueberry pomegranate juice

1 black licorice wheel, for garnish

Shake the ingredients with ice in a cocktail shaker and strain the mixture into a martini glass. Garnish with the black licorice wheel. If you're feeling playful, cut the wheel into black licorice strings and make them look like spider legs coming out of your glass!

Christmas Candy Cane Martini

Wondering what to serve your Christmas guests to get them good and relaxed? Well, we just happen to have invented the ultimate Christmas cocktail—and we challenge you to find anything more festive.

White chocolate, melted, for rim (page 16)

Crushed red peppermint hard candies, for rim

3 ounces half & half

2 ounces white chocolate liqueur

1 ounce vanilla vodka

⅛ teaspoon peppermint extract

1 candy cane, for garnish

Rim a martini glass with melted white chocolate and crushed red peppermint hard candies and set it aside. Shake the rest of the ingredients with ice in a cocktail shaker and then strain the mixture into the glass. Garnish with the candy cane.

Red Hot Christmas Sangria

Our cousin told as about this amazing Red Hots Sangria she had once at a party. We were a little skeptical but decided to invent our own recipe. To our surprise, it was actually really good! We thought given its cinnamon flavor and large party-friendly size, it would make the perfect edition to any Christmas party.

1 (750 ml) bottle red wine

2 ounces fresh lemon juice

1 lemon, cut into slices

1 orange, cut into slices

1 lime, cut into slices

1 apple, cut into slices

1 cup Red Hots

1 (one-liter) bottle ginger ale

Pour the red wine into a large pitcher or large bowl. Add the lemon juice, fruit slices, and Red Hots. Mix and refrigerate overnight. Just before serving, stir in the ginger ale. Serve in punch glasses or wine glasses, and add a few pieces of fruit for garnish to each glass.

CANDY COCKTAILS

How to Throw a Candy Cocktail Party

Now that you know how to make some awesome candy cocktails, it's time to throw your friends a cocktail party! We've got lots of DIY ideas for decorating your party and entertaining your guests. We hope that these suggestions will spark ideas of your own—get creative!

The very first step is to send your friends a candy-themed party invitation decorated with lollipops and candies!

Party Decorations

Piñatas

Candy wreaths and garlands

Candy topiaries

Candy necklace napkin holders

Candy name place holders

Candy dessert bar

Cocktail parasols

Cocktail stirrers

Tissue paper pom-poms

Party Favors

Swedish fish, foil-wrapped candy, gumballs, Lifesavers, jelly beans, conversation hearts, gumdrops, and other candies wrapped in cellophane bags and tied with colorful ribbons

Candy necklaces and bracelets

Ring Pops

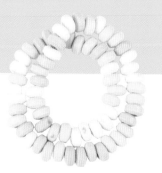

- Candy ice cream bar

- Vodka gummies on a stick

- Piñata cake

- Candy sushi

- Candy trail mix

- Dirt-y cupcakes

- Candy corn popcorn balls

- Candy "kabobs" (marshmallows, folded sour candy belts, and various gummy candies stacked on skewers)

- Chocolate-covered marshmallows on pretzel sticks, covered in colored sprinkles

- Pop Rocks–dipped chocolate-covered strawberries

Party Photo Booth

Photo booth backgrounds
(colorful streamers or gold and
silver fringe)

Candy crowns

Confetti

Party hats

Candy Necklaces

DIY Bubblegum Necklaces

Ring Pops

Formulas for Metric Conversions

Ounces to grams=multiply ounces by 28.35
Cups to liters=multiply cups by .24

METRIC EQUIVALENTS FOR WEIGHT

U.S.	Metric
1 oz	28 g
2 oz	57 g
3 oz	85 g
4 oz	113 g
5 oz	142 g
6 oz	170 g
7 oz	198 g
8 oz	227 g
16 oz (1 lb.)	454 g
2.2 lbs.	1 kilogram

METRIC EQUIVALENTS FOR VOLUME

U.S.	Metric	
⅛ tsp.	0.6 ml	—
¼ tsp.	1.2 ml	—
½ tsp.	2.5 ml	—
¾ tsp.	3.7 ml	—
1 tsp.	5 ml	—
1½ tsp.	7.4 ml	—
2 tsp.	10 ml	—
1 Tbsp.	15 ml	—
1½ Tbsp.	22 ml	—
2 Tbsp. (⅛ cup)	30 ml	1 fl. oz
3 Tbsp.	45 ml	—
¼ cup	59 ml	2 fl. oz
⅓ cup	79 ml	—
½ cup	118 ml	4 fl. oz
⅔ cup	158 ml	—
¾ cup	178 ml	6 fl. oz
1 cup	237 ml	8 fl. oz
1¼ cups	300 ml	—
1½ cups	355 ml	—
1¾ cups	425 ml	—
2 cups (1 pint)	500 ml	16 fl. oz
3 cups	725 ml	—
4 cups (1 quart)	.95 liters	32 fl. oz
16 cups (1 gallon)	3.8 liters	128 fl. oz

Acknowledgments

Writing a cocktail book was a dream of ours from the day we started our blog. After many words of discouragement from people who didn't understand our sparkly, candy-coated vision, we gave up on the idea. Then, what seemed to be out of nowhere, came an email from a literary agent. She said that she liked our blog and thought it could make a great book. We were stunned. *Who was this person? Was she legit? Was this a real agency?* In what seemed like an instant we went from dreaming about a book to actually having a book deal. Thank you, Brandi!

We have to thank our cousin, Tabitha, and our friend Amy who tirelessly tasted candy cocktail after candy cocktail until their teeth hurt and they couldn't see straight. It was a tough job, but somebody had to do it!

Flannery would like to thank her husband, Jeremy, and their daughter, Vivienne Lee, for being her biggest fans.

Katherine would like to thank her friends Tanvir and Khristina for their endless support and encouragement.

Finally, we want to thank our editor, Jordana, our book designer, Melissa, and everyone at Running Press for making this a truly amazing experience! Cheers!

Photo Credits

Photos © Steve Legato unless noted otherwise.

Cover: ©Katherine Good

p. 9 (peanut butter cup): ©Shutterstock.com/Steve Degenhardt

p. 9 (gumballs): ©Shutterstock.com/Brenda Carson

p. 10: ©Shutterstock.com/nito

p. 11 (brandy): ©Shutterstock.com/Mariyana M

p. 11 (martini): ©Shutterstock.com/Yuri Samsonov

p. 11 (julep): ©Shutterstock.com/Greg Stanfield

p. 11 (champagne): ©Shutterstock.com/Boule

p. 11 (collins): ©Shutterstock.com/Evgeny Karandaev

p. 12 (mason): ©Shutterstock.com

p. 12 (milkshake): ©Shutterstock.com/Dudaeva

p. 12 (old-fashioned): ©Shutterstock.com/Kondor83

p. 12 (wine): ©Shutterstock.com/Ninell

p. 12 (highball): ©Shutterstock.com/Palle Christensen

p. 12 (margarita): ©Shutterstock.com/Phent

p. 12 (mug): ©Shutterstock.com/Tarasyuk Igor

p. 12 (shot): ©Shutterstock.com/grafvision

p. 14 (top): ©Shutterstock.com/alex saberi

p. 14 (bottom): ©Shutterstock.com/vikiri

p. 16 (caramels): ©Shutterstock.com/urbanlight

Index

Note: Page references in *italics* indicate recipe photographs.